GW01182540

Original title:
Snow Much Drama

Author: Seraphina Caldwell
ISBN HARDBACK: 978-9916-94-204-8
ISBN PAPERBACK: 978-9916-94-205-5

The Snowball Effect

A frosty globe rolls down the street,
Pick up a few friends for a comedic feat.
It grows and grows, oh what a sight,
Make way for chaos, come join the flight!

Bananas fly in a frigid breeze,
Giggling kids throw balls with ease.
Everyone’s laughing, no time to frown,
As the snowball makes its way into town!

Crystalline Conflicts

In a world of white, where icicles swing,
Two snowmen argue, over whose hat is king.
A carrot nose, one claims is the best,
While the other insists it's his penguin vest!

A battle of wits, as snowflakes cheer,
Who will reign supreme, who will shed a tear?
Let the hilarity of winter unfold,
With frosty friendships that never grow cold!

The Intrigue of Ice

On a frozen pond, the skaters collide,
One spins and falls, the crowd can’t decide.
Is it grace or a slip, what’s making them scream?
The drama unfolds like a winter’s dream!

Polar bears watch, with looks of surprise,
As a squirrel in boots does an elaborate rise.
The intrigue spins on, what a wild show,
With giggles and gasps in the icy glow!

Frost-covered Facades

Behind frosted windows, secrets are kept,
Where yetis and elves, in their whispers, crept.
A snowball fight fades into the night,
While penguins plot all of their icy delight!

With hats on their heads and scarves flailing wide,
The neighborhood gossip is served with pride.
But laughter is louder than cold winter air,
As joy tumbles forth from this snowy affair!

Shattered Silence in White

The quiet world wears winter's crown,
A snowball fight turns calm to clown.
Giggling friends with cheeks aglow,
Launch fluffy missiles, watch them go!

A snowman wobbles, sticks in hand,
A lopsided grin, it's unplanned.
Carrot nose? More like a stick!
This frosty art is quite the trick!

Frozen Fractures

Icicles hang, a gleaming threat,
A slip on ice? You bet, you bet!
With laughter ringing, down I go,
Like a cartoon, oh what a show!

Snowflakes tumble, they twist and twirl,
One lands on my nose, what a swirl!
Pet cats leap, thinking it's prey,
While folks just grin and drift away.

Tension Beneath the Frost

A snow fort rising, battles roar,
The squirrels watch from a frozen shore.
A truce declared, we sip warm drinks,
But plotting snowball schemes, oh, what winks!

The pups dash out, tails in the air,
Chasing snowflakes without a care.
As they crash down, into a pile,
Nature's antics, making us smile!

The Drama of Falling Snowflakes

Each flake a dancer, pirouette,
Landing softly, no regret.
But wait—did I just step in goo?
My boots now lost, an epic bluuue!

Underneath that frosted veil,
The slip and slide, a comic tale.
With giggles echoing through the night,
Winter mischief, oh what a sight!

Heartbeats Beneath the Flurry

Flakes tumble down, a white parade,
Sledders and snowmen all unafraid.
A dog's pure joy, chasing after his tail,
While kids in the snowbank giggle and wail.

Frosty noses, rosy cheeks,
A snowball fight, but who peeks?
Laughter echoes in the chill,
While frozen mittens become a thrill.

Thawing Tensions

Two friends argue, who threw that ball?
One's on the roof while the other’s in thrall.
Slippery slopes lead to a slip and slide,
Both now laughing, their tempers subside.

A snowman watches with a cautious grin,
As their chilly rivalry wears thin.
Hot cocoa waits for the truce to unfold,
And all is forgotten in warmth manifold.

The Enigma of a Frozen Landscape

Footprints cover the glistening white,
Where did they go? Out of sight!
A hidden snow angel, a peekaboo game,
Mysteries bloom in a world softly tamed.

Icicles dangle like crystal swords,
As kids plot mischief, ignoring their wards.
A frost-glazed wonder, both quiet and loud,
Chasing their laughter, the snowflakes bowed.

Caught in the Cold

A hat sails off; oh, what a scene!
As gloves go flying, it's chaos pristine.
A snowman's face, one eye out of place,
Thoughts of perfection just a wild chase.

Neighbors are peeking, a curious sight,
Watching the antics of flurries and flight.
Whispers of warmth slowly break through,
While snowball chaos bids winter adieu.

Crystal Conflicts Under Moonlit Skies

In the midst of fluffy white,
A snowball flies, oh what a sight!
Two pals duel with frosty grins,
Laughter rings as the chaos spins.

Icicles dangle from rooftops high,
Sleds are racing, watch them fly!
But one crash lands, what a flop,
Echoes of giggles, they just can't stop.

The snowman wears a crooked grin,
As snowflakes dance, their playful spin.
A carrot nose with mischief made,
A head fall off—oh, what a parade!

Bunny tracks weave, a funny trace,
Tiny prints in this icy race.
At the campfire, tales inspire,
As marshmallows roast, hearts retire.

Polar Shadows and Heartfelt Dilemmas

Waddling penguins in a line,
Strut their stuff, all looking fine.
But oops! One trips and takes a slip,
In snow they tumble, a hilarious flip.

A polar bear steals a fishy feast,
While the Arctic fox watches, confused to say the least.
Chasing shadows under the low sun,
In the icy realm, the jokes never run.

Snowflakes fall, a cold cascade,
Mock battles crash, who’s unafraid?
Frolicking creatures have a ball,
As blunders happen, they laugh through it all.

Lost mittens lie in the fluffy white,
The hunt begins, what a sight!
In the chill, with laughter so bright,
Polar dramas unfold through the night.

Chill of Betrayal in the Glistening Night

Under stars, a trust unwinds,
A snowball fight blurs all lines.
Friends plot tricks, all in good cheer,
But one friend strikes, whoops! Oh dear!

Sleds collide with a comedic crash,
Giggling figures in a snowy splash.
Betrayal? Perhaps—but all in jest,
Loyalty's tested in this frosty quest.

In the moonlight, secrets are sworn,
A snowman’s hat now slightly worn.
With icy stakes and chilly glee,
Who hides behind the trees? Oh me!

The night is filled with laughter and cries,
Every misstep brings humorous sighs.
As frostbite nips and spirits rise,
This chill of drama brings joyful ties.

Frozen Fractures of the Soul

A snow angel lies, wings outstretched,
But one foolish prank leaves it wretched.
A friend lands hard, what a glare!
In frozen landscapes, do they care?

A puppy bounds through the drifting curls,
Chasing snowflakes in playful whirls.
But oops! A tumble leads to a chase,
All’s forgiven in this silly race.

Hot cocoa spills, oh what a scene,
With marshmallow fluff in between.
As laughter echoes on this frosty stroll,
These frozen fractures warm the soul.

Even in chaos, joy takes its toll,
As frosty friendships make us whole.
In winter’s grip, with hearts so light,
They frolic and stumble through the night.

Silence of Falling Flakes

Every flake that falls today,
Whispers secrets on the way.
Laughter hides in icy grooves,
While silence dances, slips, and moves.

Noses red and cheeks aglow,
Chasing friends who slip and flow.
In this world of white and cheer,
Laughter echoes loud and near.

Snowballs fly with playful aim,
A friendly fight, oh what a game!
Watch that snowman start to sway,
A tipping hat in wild dismay.

As flakes blend with all our sighs,
Laughter rummages through the skies.
Quiet drifts can’t last too long,
In this world, we all belong.

Frigid Passions

Lovebirds bundled, cozy tight,
Braving chills with hearts so bright.
Each snowflake serves as a spark,
Creating warmth from the dark.

Hot cocoa spills on winter clothes,
Underneath, true laughter flows.
Slipping skaters spin and reel,
While snowmen joke, they just can't feel.

Under stars, they will engage,
Frosty hearts set the stage.
While frozen tongues will surely freeze,
We’ll laugh about these little sleaze.

Frigid winds can’t halt the show,
Our hearts beat fast, we’ll never slow.
Every slip and fall, oh dear,
In this season, joy's sincere.

The Beauty in the Blizzard

Out in the storm, we stomp and play,
Creating chaos in a ballet.
Every flurry spun in haste,
Turns the mundane into a taste.

Chilly kisses start to freeze,
Yet laughter flows with such great ease.
Beneath each branch, there’s surprise,
Comedic moments make us rise.

Blinded by the fluffy white,
We tumble down, oh what a sight!
Even the sled dogs shake their heads,
While we write jokes on snowflakes' beds.

Snowmen grinning ear to ear,
In this wild frosty atmosphere.
With every drift, our laughter fades,
Yet winter holds our sweet charades.

Conundrums on the Ice

Icy patches gleam and shine,
Trip and fall, it’s all divine!
Twists and turns upon the rink,
With every glide, we pause and think.

Is that a penguin? No, it’s Fred!
Sailing past, he’s lightly sped.
Skates like blades, no grace in sight,
But who could care? We’re filled with light!

In this freeze, confusion reigns,
As laughter swells, it breaks the chains.
Our silly fumbles weave the fun,
In this silly race, we’re never done!

Joies and sorrows intertwine,
A winter dance; we all align.
With every slip, we find our way,
In conundrums, we choose to play.

Bitter Chill

A flake lands on my nose,
And suddenly I freeze,
With every gasp and pose,
I realize, oh please!

The landscape's quite a sight,
With drifts that daringly loom,
But watch your step tonight,
Or you'll end up in doom!

The sledders zip and zoom,
While snowmen steal the show,
Yet I just find my room,
And bake to fend off woe!

Oh, winter’s pristine charm,
Brings laughter, shivers, too,
With every chilly harm,
Comes giggles, pure and true!

Warmer Hearts

Cocoa by the fire, hot,
We share our tales so bright,
Each story burns a spot,
In frosty, cozy night.

With mittens on our hands,
We waddle like two ducks,
Building castles on sands,
Of icy, snowy plucks!

To dance in swirling flakes,
Oh joy, and laughter’s call,
When winter finally wakes,
We’re all here, standing tall!

So tie those laces tight,
And brace for every slide,
In the warmth of this night,
We take it all in stride!

Secrets Beneath the Surface

Beneath the gleaming dome,
Lies secrets yet untold,
A world, a snowy foam,
Waits for the brave and bold.

What lurks ‘neath white expanse?
Perhaps a hidden tale?
A snowball fight's fine chance,
To turn the tide and wail!

Hidden critters scheming,
Under layers of frost,
While chilly winds keep dreaming,
Of tales once thought lost!

So pack your sled with cheer,
And don that goofy grin,
For in this winter sphere,
Adventure's about to begin!

Frigid Encounters

I slipped on that slick path,
And met the ground with flair,
The snowflakes held their laugh,
As I rolled without care.

A snowball aimed with glee,
Unleashed upon my face,
'Twas a friendly decree,
In this icy, wild race!

The blizzards, quite a host,
Invite us for a round,
But oh, who’s laughing most?
When noses meet the ground!

Yet still we gather near,
In huddles, warmth to share,
For every frigid cheer,
Brings warmth to winter’s air!

The Melting Edge of Truth

As spring whispers some lies,
The ice begins to waltz,
We watch those frosty skies,
With snow-dripped, soggy faults.

Melting secrets emerge,
As puddles form their tales,
Each drop, a funny urge,
With giggles in the gales!

Oh, the slides growing slick,
A cat on ice might trip,
While laughter’s just the kick,
We cling to winter's grip!

So let the thaw begin,
With our hats fluttering high,
We laugh through thick and thin,
As the snow bids goodbye!

The Storm Within

In the sky, clouds gather fast,
A blizzard’s party, not meant to last.
The wind spins tales, oh what a show,
As socks and mittens begin to blow.

I'd grab my gear, but where's my hat?
The cat has claimed it; imagine that!
He struts around like he owns the place,
In his fluffy throne, what a funny face!

Outside the window, kids start to scream,
“Build a snowman!” in a dreamy gleam.
But as they go, the snowflakes melt,
And the winter's humor, is truly felt!

Oh, winter’s dance is one of delight,
With tumbles and slips, it’s quite a sight!
As laughter echoes, the cold winds sway,
In this wild storm, we’re here to play.

Frosty Facades

Piled high, the snow drifts near,
A house made of white, filled with cheer.
Yet under the fluff, a secret lurks,
A snowman’s hat; an old shirt that jerks.

His carrot nose, a bit askew,
Stares at the kids, like ‘What’s new?’
With eyes of coal, he starts to glare,
As mounds of snow fall in his hair.

Next door, a fort towers tall,
A battleground, oh what a brawl!
With snowballs flying, the giggles rise,
A flurry of fun, beneath gray skies.

But when it melts, how will we cope?
With soggy shoes and fading hope?
Yet for today, we laugh and glide,
In frosty facades, our joy won't slide.

The Quiet Before the Flurry

The sky hangs thick, a hush is near,
The air’s electric, full of cheer.
It’s too calm, something’s brewing,
A shifty storm, with zest pursuing.

The squirrels are twitching, what’s at stake?
They gather acorns; oh, for goodness’ sake!
With twirls and leaps, they scurry away,
Preparing for chaos, in a funny ballet.

The stillness breaks with a sudden roar,
As fluffy flakes begin to pour.
But watch your step; it’s a slippery plot,
Where kittens and kids are all that we've got!

Then off they dash like comets bright,
Into the white, what a silly sight!
The quiet's gone, let the fun erupt,
In winter's embrace, we’re happily cupped.

Echoes in the Snowdrifts

Footprints vanish, whispers of fun,
In the frosty woods, where we run.
Each splotch of mud makes a story told,
Of silly antics, and joy uncontrolled.

A tumble here, a splat there,
The snowball fights fill the chilly air.
Laughter erupts from every feat,
As snowmen wobble on shaky feet!

But look! A snow angel, perfectly made,
Kicking up snow, never to fade.
Yet soon a blizzard swirls all around,
In this winter that's silly, let's be unbound!

And when it melts, what will we say?
That winter's mischief took our breath away.
The echoes linger, we'll always know,
In the heart of winter, there's magic in snow.

A Blizzard of Emotions

A flake fell down, a dance on the air,
Turning my hat into winterwear.
With all this chill, my nose turns bright,
Is it just me, or is this a snowball fight?

The neighbor's dog, a blizzard's foe,
Chasing snowflakes, oh what a show!
He leaps and tumbles, all in glee,
Meanwhile, I trip on a mound, oh me!

Boots soaked through, am I getting old?
Slipping on ice – it's always bold.
Giggles echo, as I lose my grip,
Come join the circus, take a wild trip!

As snowmen rise with their carrot noses,
They stand guard while winter dozes.
A blizzard of laughter, a flurry of cheer,
In this winter wonderland, we have no fear!

Whirlwind of Winter's Whispers

A scarf around my neck, it’s quite a sight,
Flapping like banners, oh what a fright!
I sipped my cocoa, feeling so grand,
Until a snowball came, thrown by a hand!

Children laugh, their cheeks rosy red,
Covering my head with snow, it’s widespread!
A whirlwind of giggles, all in the air,
Forgetting my worries, without a care.

Little boots crunch, making prints in the white,
“Let’s build a fort!” they yell with delight.
While I attempt to craft some walls,
My structure crumbles, like winter falls!

From cozy indoors to the chilly outside,
Where laughter and chaos happily collide.
Life is a joke when you’re coated in frost,
In this whirlpool of winter, never a loss!

Frostbitten Fantasies

Frosty mornings bring dreams of play,
A snowflake queen in a grand ballet.
But wait, I slipped, oh what a sight,
Maybe I’ll stick to warm cocoa tonight!

The snowman grins, a goofy chap,
Wearing my hat, how could I nap?
He’s got my sunglasses, my shades so bright,
Now he’s rockin' them, posing just right!

Snow angels flap in the powdery white,
With wings so grand, they'll take to flight.
But suddenly sinking, I find no grace,
Just a flurry of giggles in this winter race.

Frostbitten dreams, oh what a thrill,
Shivering laughter gives everyone a chill.
A whimsical world, where fun has no bounds,
In this frosty fairyland, joy abounds!

Pale Shadows in the Snow

Pale shadows dance as the moonlight glows,
Emerging from laughter, where the cold wind blows.
With marshmallows flying, hot cocoa spills,
Each winter adventure, a challenge that thrills.

Tiny footprints lead to the frozen creek,
Marvelous stories of winter we seek.
But with every leap, there comes a plop,
Into the cold water—oh, help, please stop!

The trees wear blankets, snowflakes galore,
A shoveling saga that's never a bore.
While I fight snow, it fights back with style,
Rolling down hills with the goofiest smile.

Pale shadows unite in mischief and cheer,
Creating memories that stay ever near.
In this land of whispers and frosty delight,
Life's just a comedy, wrapped up tight!

Fractured Reflections of Winter

Frosty flakes dance on my nose,
While a snowball flies, and a scream arose.
Laughter echoes in the chilly air,
As I slip and slide without a care.

Snowmen wobble, their faces askew,
One lost a carrot, they haven’t a clue.
My dog thinks he's a sled on four legs,
Chasing his tail, he’s lost all his eggs.

Hot cocoa warms my frozen hands,
While I plot my next snowball stands.
Children giggle, and adults retreat,
When we launch surprise attacks in the street.

As night falls, we watch the stars twinkle,
My friend trips over a very small sprinkle.
We collapse in laughter, a glorious sight,
Oh, winter's a hoot in the frosty night!

Twilight of the Tundra

Under a blanket of shimmering white,
The penguins march, no end in sight.
They waddle and wobble, oh what a show,
One slips on ice, the rest laugh, 'No!'

Frosty breath if we take a chance,
We trip through snow in a silly dance.
A snowman spies from a nearby hill,
With button eyes, he's got quite a thrill.

My friend's hair sparkles, like a disco ball,
As we throw snow like it's a free-for-all.
With every toss, we lose a glove,
Winter's a party, like push comes to shove.

The moon peeks down, a spotlight shines,
We're building dreams from icy designs.
So let the drama keep on its way,
In this winter wonderland of play!

Tensions Frozen in Time

When flakes begin to dance and spin,
Neighbors glare, where to begin?
Slippery paths and a sledding spree,
Who will laugh, who'll fall, and see?

Hot cocoa spills on wooly mitts,
Glib remarks and playful hits.
As winter wraps us in its charm,
We bicker, freeze, but mean no harm.

Snowmen argue whose nose is best,
Carrot or stick, it's a funny quest.
A snowball fight on the front lawn,
Laughter erupts as fray goes on.

In the quiet, emotions grow,
Breath catches with each frost’s show.
Yet we laugh through the icy fray,
With frozen smiles, we dance and play.

The Lament of a Frost-Laden Heart.

A snowplow's roar disrupts the peace,
While hearts glide on, seeking release.
Chilly charms in a winter's glow,
Yet love feels tangled in the snow.

Mittens hug hands meant to be warm,
But sleds collide, no hint of charm.
Lovers argue on where to steer,
Each puff of breath a frosty cheer.

Romantic dinners turned cold as ice,
Hearts thaw out, but love's not precise.
Lost in laughter, we both pretend,
That winter's drama won't ever end.

So bundle up, embrace the chill,
With each slip, we climb up the hill.
In this fresh dance, our warmth we'll find,
And melt away what froze our mind.

Whispers of Winter's Veil

Under layers of white, secrets lie,
Whispers of snowflakes as they fly.
Friends gather ‘round, eyes bright with glee,
Each topped mug held for all to see.

A snow fort shields against ice cold words,
Impromptu battles, laughter like birds.
The drama unfolds, as two lovers fight,
Over which sledding hill gives the best flight.

Yet giggles echo in the frosted air,
While frozen toes become our dare.
Who will crack the ice first with grace?
In the chill, we all find our place.

Hey, don’t slip! Watch where you stand!
Bound together by snow, hand in hand.
This winter’s drama, so wild and bright,
Leaves us laughing come morning light.

Frosted Confessions

In the freeze of night, confessions bloom,
Chilly air full of laughter, not gloom.
Under the stars, secrets flit about,
What was cold, now warms with a shout.

A snow angel’s heart begins to race,
As frosty souls find a warmer place.
Slipping and sliding on frozen thrills,
Captured moments embrace the chills.

Outrageous tales of past winters bold,
While frosted memories silently unfold.
We muse on the slips, the falls, and the fun,
In this winter’s play, all our hearts are spun.

With each giggle, the frost starts to fade,
Organic warmth in this grand charade.
So raise your mugs, let the laughter fly,
For in winter's grip, friendships can’t lie.

Frost-tinged Betrayals

Flakes fall, a silent prank,
Puppies leap, oh what a tank.
Sleds collide, and laughter spreads,
Who knew winter hid such dreads?

Chill fools rush to make a snowman,
Lopsided giants, what a plan!
A carrot nose, but wait, oh dear!
He’s lost his head, so full of cheer!

Snowballs fly, who'll take a hit?
Loyal pals in icy skit.
Betrayed by warmth, they slip and fall,
In frosty glee, we laugh through all.

Then icy winds, they start to howl,
Chasing us with a frosty growl.
But in the fun, we find our way,
Winter's antics come out to play.

Tempest of Tranquility

A blanket white, so calm at first,
Yet chaos brews, a snowball burst.
Children giggle, frolicking free,
In this frozen jubilee.

Carrot noses, hats askew,
Snowmen grinning, who knew?
“Build me taller!” one child yells,
Yet down it goes, like ringing bells.

A shovel slipped, a grand display,
Into a drift, oh what a ballet!
Laughter echoes through the trees,
In these storms, we find our ease.

As snowflakes dance in blizzard's might,
We dodge and weave, what a sight!
Yet in this tempest, joy stands tall,
With friends around, we break the fall.

Surreal Silence

The world hushed under frosty grace,
But slip on ice, and it's a race!
A thump, a laugh, the quiet breaks,
Who knew winter could cause such shakes?

A snow angel, oh what a scene,
Wings of white, a cushy dream.
Yet beneath it, a hidden thunk,
Did someone leave their old junk?

Silent glens with secrets to keep,
Yet one lost boot, oh what a leap!
Chasing the laughter, hear it ring,
Even in cold, we find our zing.

As the stars pierce the wintry night,
We stack the snow, a majestic sight.
With each slip and fall, we wear our crowns,
In surreal silence, laughter drowns.

Empires of Ice

In kingdoms forged by chilly hands,
Playful battles in frozen lands.
Twisted towers reach for the sky,
But wait, who made that slip and cry?

Sno-cones from icicles, who'll take a bite?
Rumbling laughter, a wild delight.
As snowmen frown at battles lost,
In these frosty wars, we pay the cost.

Belly flops in powdered hills,
Spinning rounds, oh what thrills.
A crown of frost, we rule the day,
In this empire, joy finds a way.

So raise your mugs of cocoa warm,
To those who weather every storm.
Empires of ice, with hearts so free,
In every laugh, there's unity.

Crystal Traces of Turmoil

Tiny flakes fall from above,
Creating chaos, what a shove!
Kids in jackets, boots so loud,
Tumbling down, it draws a crowd.

Sleds collide, a snowball flies,
Laughter echoes, oh what a prize!
A snowy fortress, quite the sight,
Defending kingdoms, ready to fight.

A dog appears, on a mission bold,
To steal the hat, so high, so cold!
Chasing tails, in a dizzy spin,
Winter mischief, let the games begin.

As daylight fades, the chill sets in,
Hot cocoa waits, let the giggles win.
Crystal traces, all around,
In this whirlwind, fun is found.

Glistening Deceptions

A pristine hill, white and bright,
But hidden bumps bring quite a fright.
With every slide, a chance to flop,
Glistening deceptions, who’ll take a drop?

A snowman stands, all proud and tall,
But watch it wobble, wait for the fall!
Carrot-nose spins, whoops, there it goes,
As giggles burst, everyone knows.

The trees wear coats of shiny frost,
Yet underneath, it's fun that’s lost.
A playful pup leaps with glee,
Racing through mystery!

The sun peeks out, the game’s not done,
As shoelaces tangle, a slippery run.
In this kingdom of white, we play to beguile,
Glistening deceptions, all with a smile.

Fateful Flakes

Each flake falls as if it knows,
They land on noses, and wiggle toes.
With every gust, they swirl in flight,
Creating tales of pure delight.

A stumble here, a tumble there,
Laughter erupts, fills the cold air.
Fateful flakes, just watch them dance,
Every slip leads to a chance!

A fort built high, in defense we shout,
Snowballs flying, no time to pout!
Frosty friendships, bonds are made,
In this white wonderland, plans are laid.

As evening approaches, shadows grow,
But the fun continues, with lots of snow.
Fateful flakes, oh what a spree,
In this winter chaos, joy runs free.

Hidden Crystals of Conflict

Beneath the drifts, a truth is veiled,
As snowmen clash, and laughter wailed.
Hidden crystals of what’s to come,
In the midst of fun, beware the bum!

A snowball flies, a gentle throw,
But watch for shields, and dodge them low.
With every fling, a new surprise,
Hidden conflict beneath the skies.

Sister screams, “That’s not so fair!”
Brothers laugh, without a care.
A game erupts, in soft white bliss,
Conflict’s laughter, they can’t resist.

With dusk they sit, snowflakes chase,
In every drop, is friendship’s grace.
Hidden crystals of joy collide,
In this snowy world, let's take a ride.

Treacherous Trails

Watch your step on frosty ground,
One slip and you'll spin around!
Making snow angels feels so bright,
Till you land on a snowbank, what a sight!

Sledding down a hill with glee,
But wait, where did I leave my tea?
A snowball flies, my aim is true,
I hit the dog, oh whoops, it's you!

Icicles hanging, sharp as knives,
A winter wonderland comes alive,
But falling off a toboggan, oh dear,
Can't tell if I'm laughing or in fear!

In boots so big, I waddle like a fool,
Each step I take feels like an uphill duel,
Yet with every slip and slide anew,
My heart dances in this snowy brew!

Silent Storms

Outside my window, flakes drift down,
Each one a tiny, swirling clown.
Hot cocoa spills as I try to sip,
And suddenly I'm on a sugar trip!

A snowman stares with eyes of coal,
But I doubt he’s got a warming soul.
His carrot nose points to the sky,
Wouldn’t it be funny if he learned to fly?

Powdered chaos swirls all around,
With each gust of wind, I’m ground-bound.
My umbrella flips, I’m caught in a whirl,
And all I can do is laugh and twirl!

Laughter echoes through the frozen trees,
As I dive in deeper, feeling the freeze.
It's a chill that tickles, a chill that pleases,
Winter’s comedy never ceases!

Frosty Interludes

Chilling winds sneak through the door,
While scarves and mittens fall on the floor.
A hot bath planned for this bleak day,
But I forgot I left the faucet to spray!

Tiny flakes begin to dance,
With every shiver, I take a chance.
A game of dodge with dripping icicles,
My dodging skills? More like sickles!

The kitchen’s a mess, flour in my hair,
Baked goods? More like a winter scare.
With every pie that starts to flop,
I hear my neighbors cheer and hop!

Yet through this chaos and frosty play,
Laughter warms up the coldest day.
A mishap here, a giggle there,
Winter's joy has filled the air!

Echoes of Icebound Truths

In the hush of night, the world feels strange,
Icicles singing, oh what a change!
But with each note, I start to see,
That winter's serenade is flying free.

A snowball fight breaks the calm delight,
Laughter erupts, a glorious sight.
Though shivers dance, I'm filled with cheer,
As friends become foes, yet we persevere!

The moon reflects on silent white,
While I trip over a snowman, what a fright!
Yet through the giggles and playful chase,
There's joy in winter's icy embrace.

So raise your mugs, toast to the scene,
Where laughter reigns, if not serene.
In the heart of winter, we thrive and glow,
With echoes of frost, let the fun overflow!

Tangle in the Tundra

In the tundra, laughter cheer,
A snowball fight, oh my dear.
Bunnies dodging, slipping fast,
While penguins waddle—what a blast!

Sleds collide, a comic scene,
In fluffy coats, we dance and preen.
With every tumble, giggles sound,
As we fall over, hugs abound!

Chasing snowflakes, running wild,
With hats askew, we're like a child.
The winter air, it sparkles bright,
In this chilly, frosty fight!

So grab your pals, don’t delay,
In this tundra, we shall play.
The fun won’t stop, let’s raise a cheer,
For tangled joy is truly near!

Layers of Frosted Lies

Beneath the drifts, a secret grows,
A tale of frost and winter's prose.
Whispers swirl like snowflakes fair,
All tangled up in winter’s snare.

A snowman’s scarf tells tales so bold,
Of how he danced in nights of cold.
With carrot noses, falsehoods reign,
His frozen smile hides the pain.

Elves in mittens, hoarding facts,
Inventing stories, crafting acts.
Oh, winter's stage, with costumes bright,
We laugh at truths that take to flight!

So when you tread in winter’s glow,
Beware the tales that start to flow.
For under layers, often lies,
Are funny truths in frosty skies!

The Art of Frosted Chaos

Amidst the flakes, a wild ballet,
As sleds and laughter dance away.
With hats askew and boots in tow,
We spin in chaos, don’t you know?

The friendly dog, a furry thief,
Steals winter’s joys without a grief.
He zooms through trails, a goofy sight,
While we collapse, it feels so right!

With mischief brewing, snowballs fly,
As giggles bubble up to the sky.
We trip and tumble, hold our sides,
In frosted chaos, joy abides!

So grab your friends, don’t hesitate,
Join the madness, it’s never too late.
In winter’s grip, we'll paint the air,
With funny tales, let down your hair!

Penned in Winter

In winter’s chill, the stories blend,
Of snowmen, snowballs, and silly bends.
Each tale a laugh, a frosty delight,
Where every turn sparks sheer joy, outright!

With cups of cocoa, we gather ‘round,
Listening close to the tales abound.
Of penguins wearing socks on feet,
And dancing sleds that can’t be beat!

The quills of winter take to flight,
As scribbles turn to pure delight.
In a land of frosted mirth we find,
Pranks and giggles of every kind.

So pen your joy, let laughter flow,
In winter’s grip, let happiness grow.
For every giggle, every rhyme,
Is the magic of a snowy time!

Icicles and Heartstrings

The icicles hang, a jagged show,
My heartstrings tug, oh what a glow.
They glisten like teeth in a snowy grieve,
While ice puns slip in, who can believe?

The snowflakes dance, a swirling spree,
Each soft landing, a comedy.
I slip and slide with grace unplanned,
As laughter erupts, I'll take a stand!

The flurries tickle like playful birds,
My winter coat’s filled with silly words.
I chase a snowman, he runs away,
With a carrot nose that's here to stay!

Who knew this chill could spark such glee?
A frosty world of pure esprit.
With every patch of white on the ground,
The hilarity seems to know no bounds.

A Chill in the Air

A chill rushes in, with whispers bold,
It frosts my cheeks, turns warm to cold.
The squirrels scamper, their antics grand,
Making mischief, by winter's hand.

"Watch your step!" my friend jokingly quips,
As we navigate through icy trips.
I tumble down in a bundled mess,
Laughter erupts, what a frosty jest!

The snowball fights ignite the fun,
With slippery moves, we're on the run.
Each throw misfires, a comical scene,
As snowmen crumble, life feels like a dream!

So grab your mittens, come join the cheer,
For the winter's chill, we hold so dear.
We'll forge funny tales in this frosty air,
Creating memories that we can share.

Crystal Confrontations

In a world of white, come take a look,
Where snowflakes gossip like an open book.
An argument starts, the flakes take flight,
“Who’s the sparkliest?” a lacy fight!

I venture out in boots too tight,
To join the brawl on a chilly night.
Doughy mittens full of playful spite,
My laughter echoes, a pure delight.

The frozen ground is a slippery stage,
With flaring tempers, we act our age.
Yet, as we tumble, our grumps dissolve,
In this crystal drama, problems revolve.

The sky a canvas, stars play along,
While heaving chests burst into song.
A magnificent clash, all full of cheer,
In icy encounters we hold so dear.

Winter’s Embers

With frost on the windows, we gather in,
A flicker of warmth breaks out from within.
Hot cocoa sips turn into snorts,
As marshmallows dive in our snowy courts.

The fireplace crackles with stories to tell,
Of wintery mishaps, oh can’t you tell?
A plump rabbit hops, then slips on the floor,
In a fuzzy delight, we just beg for more!

A fireplace’s glow, with laughter rings,
Echoes of winter and all that it brings.
With each joyful story from days gone by,
The embers of fun keep us laughing high.

So here in the warmth, let’s chuckle and cheer,
For every cold winter's true camaraderie here.
With friends all around, who needs a king?
Let joy be the crown that our hearts can bring!

Entangled in White

Frolic in fluff, a dance so divine,
Pants upon pants, this snow, it does shine.
My head’s stuck in wayward drifts, oh dear,
Laughter erupts, where's my sled, I fear.

A penguin parade in my front yard,
Wobbling around, it's all just too hard.
Snowballs are flying, I duck with a scream,
Who knew winter could be such a meme?

Mittens in hand, but where is the glove?
This fluffy fiasco, I’ll never get love.
Chasing my dog, he’s buried in snow,
He digs and he digs, oh, what a show!

Hot cocoa spills, a marshmallow fight,
We’re lost in the chaos, what a delight!
So here’s to the laughter among chilly bights,
Entangled in white, oh, what a sight!

Winter’s Heavy Heart

A shoveling saga begins with a sigh,
My back feels like lead, I can’t even fly.
Snowflakes may dazzle, but oh, what a chore,
Why does winter always beg for more?

Slipping and sliding, we’re at a standstill,
Footprints like art, but oh, what a thrill!
I’ve lost my right boot, it’s stuck in a mound,
Winter’s heavy heart is where I am bound.

Ice on the windows paints scenes of despair,
I swear I just saw a snowman with flair.
Grumpy old neighbors hurling their threats,
A snowball Aphrodite, he’ll surely regret!

Yet giggles erupt in this wacky white land,
With each frosty blunder, we take a strong stand.
Who cares if my face is all frosted and red?
It’s the funny mishaps that stick in my head!

Unraveled at Zero Degrees

I step out the door, it's a slippery race,
On socks that resemble a high-speed chase.
Zero degrees, but my heart starts to thaw,
With each silly stumble, I’m left in awe.

Snowmen in hats that are two sizes too small,
Their crooked little smiles just make me fall.
Doesn’t matter the cold, we’re crafting with glee,
While sleds seek revenge in a snow-laden spree!

Frosty front yards transform into slides,
Neighbors all laughing, no need for pride.
I tumble headfirst, hands waving all ‘round,
Unraveled chaos as we spin on the ground.

Hot chocolate spills from my cup with a splatter,
Yet all that I see is the wild fun chatter.
Laughter in layers, what a winter’s tease,
Unraveled at zero, oh, how we freeze!

A Veil of Winter Whispers

Under the blankets of white fluffy fluff,
Sledding sounds joyous, but it’s still quite rough.
With whispers of winter, I tumble and roll,
Gazebos like igloos grace each tiny stroll.

A snowball conspiracy brews near the fence,
What’s better than laughter? It all makes such sense!
My nose is now rosy, my cheeks look like beets,
But playing in powder, I find it all sweet.

Snowflakes like confetti, it sparkles and glows,
We dance in the flakes, and our happiness shows.
A snowman with style, he’s tipped at the chin,
Waving goodnight, as winter begins.

From snow forts of laughter to tussles anew,
Each moment we share feels warm and true blue.
So here’s to the whispers, the giggles, the cheer,
Draped in a veil, winter brings us all near!

Moonlight on a Winter's Tale

Under the moon, the snowflakes dance,
Like clumsy kids in a wild romance.
Frosty giggles fill the air,
As snowmen strike a silly dare.

Chasing shadows through the night,
One trips and starts a feathery flight.
Laughter echoes, a joyful sound,
In this winter wonderland, fun is found.

With twisty paths and icy slips,
Everyone tries to do cool flips.
A snowball flies, a hat takes flight,
In the winter's frosty delight.

So let's embrace this frozen play,
Where every stumble brightens the day.
Together we'll weave tales so absurd,
In moonlight's glow, our laughter heard.

Encased in Ice

Wrapped up tight in blankets of white,
The world transforms, a comical sight.
Parks become playgrounds, oh what glee,
With snowdrifts calling out to me.

Penguins waddle on slippery slopes,
Attempting stunts with frosty hopes.
Sideways falls, and oh what a show,
In this icy theatre, pure fun we'll sow.

The trees wear crowns of glittering frost,
Every branch a story, never lost.
A squirrel skates on a frozen pond,
As giggles echo, a joyous bond.

"Watch me jump!"—a brave friend screams,
Into the drifts, they land in dreams.
So cheers to the frosty surprises ahead,
Where laughter blooms as we forge new threads.

Whispers in the Wind

In the winter's breath, whispers play,
As mischief-makers frolic away.
Snowflakes giggle in their descent,
Covering missteps, intent unbent.

A snowman's hat flies off in delight,
As children chase it under moonlight.
Their laughter trails like twinkling stars,
Whirling and twirling, this fun is ours.

Cold fingers grasp at fleeting dreams,
While frosty air is bursting at the seams.
With every slip, our spirits soar,
In this wild winter, we're asking for more.

The wind carries tales of the shenanigans done,
As chimneys puff, we huddle for fun.
So let the winds carry our cheer,
In this chilling play, we have no fear.

The Chill of Unsaid Words

In the stillness, a chuckle brews,
As frosty breath seems to amuse.
Each missed word, a snowball toss,
In this winter, we’re the boss.

Friendships bloom under icicle skies,
With secret snickers and playful sighs.
Tangled thoughts in the frosty air,
Turn into laughter, a funny affair.

As we huddle, stories unfold,
Of silly mishaps and secrets told.
Every uneasy glance, a comedic beat,
Creating memories that can't be beat.

So here we sit, the chill wrapped tight,
Sharing whispers that feel just right.
In the snowy stillness, we find our way,
A warmth in winter’s bizarre ballet.

Tempest of Heartbeats in a Winter's Tale

Flakes flutter down like ghosts in flight,
While snowmen giggle on snowy height.
Snowball fights spark laughter and glee,
As icicles hang like chandeliers, you see.

Frosty breath puffs in cheerful displays,
Kids tumble and fall in a frosty ballet.
With mittened hands, we toss all the pain,
In this playful dance where joy is the gain.

Yet under the fluff, there's churning around,
Hearts race in secret, it's chaos profound.
Amidst fluffy layers, a crush does ignite,
Like a sleigh ride gone wild in the night.

So grab your hot cocoa, let’s make s'mores bright,
Chasing our laughs 'neath the moon's silver light.
In this winter wonder, let’s flutter and fly,
With a tempest of heartbeats and frosty sky.

Whirlwind of Emotions in Crystal Light

Glittering flakes dance in the moon’s embrace,
While cheeks turn rosy in this joyous race.
Laughter bubbles up, a thrilling delight,
In this winter game of hearts taking flight.

A sled goes careening, laughs fill the air,
'Til one poor soul lands without a care.
The shouts and the giggles, a wintery crew,
Unravel emotions as bright as the blue.

With every snow angel, hopes soar and glide,
Secret glances exchanged, with hearts open wide.
Beneath frosty layers, confusion does brew,
In this whirlwind of feelings, oh what will we do?

A snowman winks, with a crooked old smile,
While we slip on ice, and go tumbling a mile.
But wrapped in this chaos, we all find our light,
In a crystal-white world, you’re my laughter tonight.

A Biting Breeze of Unsaid Words

The chill in the air bites like teasing remarks,
As each breath clouded tells secrets to sparks.
In frosty silence, a heartbeats away,
Where laughter and longing make the sweetest bouquet.

Bundled in scarves, we venture outside,
Where snowflakes twirl like a boisterous ride.
Playful banter hides hints in between,
As we navigate feelings, both silly and green.

Each snowball hurled, an unspoken plea,
A playful nudge to reveal what we see.
Under the twinkle of stars that glow bright,
A biting chill masks what’s warm with delight.

Then giggles erupt with each misfired shot,
In this whimsical fight, we get tangled in thought.
Amidst all the frost, our hearts intertwine,
In this biting breeze, could love be divine?

Beneath the Ice, a Turmoil Grows

Under the surface, where stillness may lie,
There’s a ruckus unfolding, hidden from eye.
With ice skates slipping, we twirl and we spin,
But what’s underneath? Oh, the drama within!

As figure skaters swirl, we watch in dismay,
Who knew that the slip would steal hearts away?
With skates on the ice, our hearts pump and race,
For each little tumble feels like a fate chase.

Frostbite’s a challenge, but so is this show,
Where laughter erupts in a flamboyant flow.
In snowy revivals, amidst laughter we find,
That beneath the frost, we’re all griefs entwined.

So let’s dance on the ice, with humor our shield,
And into the chaos, our hearts shall not yield.
For beneath all the layers, turmoil can glow,
In this fanciful winter where friendship will grow.

Whispers of the Winter Storm

If snowflakes could giggle, they'd dance in the air,
Chasing off chill with a whimsical flair.
But I slipped on a patch, my pride took a dive,
While snowmen looked on, as if they'd contrived.

The squirrels laughed wildly, their cheeks full of snacks,
While I built a snow fort, complete with some cracks.
A snowball flew past me, my aim was quite lame,
And I ended up face-first, the ground said my name.

A penguin in goggles just waddled on by,
With dreams of the tropics, he let out a sigh.
While frostbitten fingers went numb on the phone,
To capture this magic, oh how it has grown!

Yet every misstep is a tale to regale,
Like slipping on ice, or a sudden snow gale.
In winter's embrace, I find joy in the fall,
For life is a circus; I just join the brawl.

Frosted Whispers and Hidden Scars

The frost on the window paints pictures of glee,
While I toss snowballs that miss targets, you see.
The dog joins the fray, his joy off the charts,
While I trip on the steps and fall flat on my parts.

The snowmen conspired, a summit was held,
Their eyes made of buttons, their secrets compelled.
But behind frosted smiles, I swear I could hear,
Laughter that echoed, both silly and clear.

A blizzard of giggles wraps ‘round like a hug,
While I sip hot cocoa — it’s sweet like a bug.
But then in a flash, I slip on a skate,
And vanish mid-air — oh, it’s never too late!

With icicles dangling, like spikes made of glee,
The winter’s a stage, and I’m sure you can see.
With every mishap, I create my own art,
In this frosty theater, plays melt from the heart.

The Icy Heart's Conundrum

In a world wrapped in blankets of white fluffy fluff,
I ponder the mysteries — do we ever get tough?
As icicles drop and my nose starts to freeze,
I can’t help but chuckle at nature’s unease.

A snow angel made, but I look like a flop,
Flippers and flounders, I just cannot stop.
A twist and a tumble, my balance did fade,
While the neighbors all laugh at my snow-laden charade.

The snowflakes tease gently, like friends on a spree,
Creating their magic, and dancing with glee.
But wait — there's a storm brewing up in the sky,
And I scramble indoors, saying “No, don’t let it fly!”

Yet each drizzled flake carries laughter and grace,
With winter’s own tricks, oh, I revel in space.
In the heart of the chaos, the cold and the chill,
I find it's the zany that gives me a thrill.

Chilling Echoes Beneath the Stars

Beneath swirling snowflakes that whisper and tease,
I strut through the night like a wintertime breeze.
With each crunching step, a dance of delight,
As the stars twinkle softly, oh what a sight!

The moon casts a glow on the cats in the snow,
Who pounce at the shadows as if on a show.
But I'm caught in the chaos, my mittens too tight,
As I tumble and tumble, oh what a sight!

A snow fort of dreams, the battleground's set,
My friends call me wacky; I'm not placing bet.
With frozen respect to the ice-capped abyss,
Every whoosh of the flakes is a wintertime kiss.

As giggles bounce high, in this frost-bitten land,
I'm the queen in the chaos with a snowball in hand.
Though frosty and funny, each moment's a play,
In this whimsical winter, we laugh all the way.

Winter's Grasp: A Tangle of Reticence

In winter’s clutch, we skitter and slide,
A snowman’s hat, our careful pride.
The sledding hill’s a slippery fate,
As snowflakes fall, we just can’t wait.

Boots lined up, a colorful row,
My friend has fallen—oh, what a show!
With laughter loud, we create a scene,
What a sight, the snow is pristine!

But deep beneath the frosty glow,
There lie secrets that we all know.
A snowball fight veers off the trail,
Now feelings mixed, we start to bail.

We hide our blushes, pretend we’re fine,
As snowmen wink and toast with wine.
Such winter tales, we craft and spin,
Amid a chill, we laugh within.

An Avalanche of Secrets in a Frosty Haven

In frosty woods, away we roam,
Where whispers linger, a hidden dome.
Each snowflake tells a tale or two,
Of furtive stares and giggles that flew.

The trees are frost-kissed, standing tall,
Yet who can tell if they're having a ball?
Upon a hill, we dare to glide,
Then tumble down in a clumsy slide.

With every laugh, a secret bestowed,
A hidden truth on this icy road.
We build a fort both slick and grand,
Yet inside lies a giggle-duel plan!

As snowballs fly, our worries melt,
In frosty fun, all grudges dealt.
This winter wonder holds joy and jest,
In frosty havens, we find our best.

Icy Paths of Reconciliation

We skated through this glistening maze,
Chasing our dreams in a frosty daze.
But slip we did, oh what a sight,
A dance of limbs in this snowy light.

Each icy path brings laughter and woes,
As friendships patch on slippery toes.
From snowdrift falls to snowball gain,
Reconciliation through snowy pain.

A misplaced throw sends secrets flying,
In icy laughter, no need for crying.
What once was stashed now flutters free,
On icy paths, it’s us—just we.

So bring your mittens, let’s mend today,
In winter's play, we’ll find our way.
A tangle of frolic, fun’s the goal,
In this chilly dance, we share our soul.

The Frigid Air of Hidden Truths

With winter’s breath, the truth runs cold,
In frosty air, our secrets unfold.
Behind frosted panes, we try to hide,
The tales of woe that tear inside.

A snowball flung, a giggle erupts,
In frigid air, no one interrupts.
Yet whispered words fly with the flurries,
As laughter dances in playful flurries.

We trudge through drifts, our feet like lead,
In the hush of snow, can we be misled?
With each slip and fall, we break the ice,
Truths in our hearts, a fragile price.

So let's embrace this winter light,
In frozen mirth, we’ll make it right.
For every truth told, new laughter blooms,
In the frigid air, our joy consumes.

The Frostbite of Forgotten Promises

Once promised to help, now it's just me,
Caught in an avalanche of sheer apathy.
Where did you go, oh friend of mine?
Lost in the drifts, sipping hot brine.

I texted you twice, but no sign appears,
While snowflakes fall, I battle my fears.
My sled lies unused, it’s gone all to waste,
Guess winter's best buddies aren’t quick to taste.

With frostbitten toes and a frown on my face,
I build a snowman with utmost grace.
Except he's just there, a silent gloom,
With eyes made of coal and no room for boom.

So here I am, on this snowy spree,
Creating drama with cups of cold tea.
Next time, dear friend, no breaking the vow,
Let’s build a snow fortress, we’ll figure it out somehow.

Shivers of Longing in a White Embrace

Caught in a blizzard, my heart takes flight,
Wishing for warmth, but I'm lonely tonight.
The flakes swirl around me, a swirling parade,
Of memories lost in this winter charade.

Thought of a dance in the crisp winter air,
But it’s just me and a snowman, eerie and bare.
“Let it go!” I shout as he stares in response,
This chilly romance is completely ensconced.

Every snowflake that falls seems to tease,
Longing for laughter, or maybe some cheese.
But here I am stuck with my frozen delight,
In this frosted tale, where I shiver and bite.

Yet somehow I smile, as I stumble and fall,
Creating my own kind of fun winter ball.
With each frosty flake, there’s a twinge of glee,
Finding humor in woes, that’s the spirit of me!

A Dilemma Wrapped in Winter's Cloak

Dressed up warmly but feeling the chill,
Tripped on my boots—oh, what a thrill!
Every step taken, a dance of disgrace,
Holding back laughter in this slippery place.

My dog zooms on, with utter delight,
While I'm here tumbling, oh what a sight!
Who knew winter games could be such a mess?
An ice skating routine turns into pure stress.

On a snow-covered hill, I tried to race,
But the sled flew off, I lost all my grace.
Wrapped in thick layers, I slip and slide,
With each frosty moment, I wear my pride.

So here's to the madness, the winter's great scheme,
A dilemma that dances in frosty moonbeams.
Laughter rings out in this white wonderland,
For every flop, there's a giggle at hand.

The Subtle Drama of Frost-Kissed Woes

In a world of white, where the crows seem to dance,
I trip over snow—it's just my luck, perhaps.
With every cold puff, drama starts to unfold,
An epic journey on this canvas of cold.

Please pass the hot cocoa, it’s essential you see,
With marshmallows floating like airships to me.
The wind whispers secrets that tickle my nose,
In this theatrical chaos, anything goes.

Fluffy flakes land on my clueless old hat,
And the snowman I built is just having a chat.
He tells me my struggles are part of the fun,
As we laugh at ourselves under bright winter sun.

So I’ll bristle and shiver in this chilly play,
Embracing the laughter that follows my sway.
For life’s little dramas will always unfold,
Wrapped in winter’s charm, where the stories are told.

Winter's Veil: Masked Intentions

In the frosty air, joys collide,
Footprints gather, side by side.
A snowball flies, a sneaky throw,
Laughter erupts as senses glow.

Hide behind the trees, take aim,
Beware the mittens, fierce the game.
Orange hats bob, a comical sight,
All's fair in love, and winter's bite.

The shovels clash, a duel of cheer,
Who will falter, who will steer?
Giggles echo through puffs of breath,
In this chill, we dance with death.

As winter wraps us in its white,
Who knew we'd fight with such delight?
Masked intentions in every throw,
In this land, absurdity flows.

The Battle of Warmth and Frost

A cozy fire, but there's a chill,
Socks and mitts are lost, but still,
I guard my cocoa, mug in hand,
While frosty fingers roam the land.

Hats on heads, a preposterous sight,
Laughter mingles with the pale moonlight.
A gust comes sneaking, with a whoosh,
Sleds collide in a snowy swoosh.

The wind declares an icy war,
While cups are filled on every floor.
Outside, a snowman, tall and proud,
But dreams of warmth feel like a cloud.

So come, gather 'round, let's share a smile,
As winter prattles on for a while.
Together we ride this comedic wave,
In warmth and frost, our hearts we save.

Errant Flurries and Fateful Encounters

A flurry whirls, a twist of fate,
I dodge a snowball, it's a slippery state.
Friends are laughing, all in good cheer,
As winter's dance draws everyone near.

A cat runs by, all fluff and grace,
In this wild game, it's hard to chase.
The snowflakes tease, they tumble down,
Muffling giggles from every town.

We trip and slip, a clumsy brigade,
With every tumble, plans are remade.
Allies found in a war of delight,
In each playful throw, we find our light.

So gather 'round through glimmers and glee,
Together we weave this funny spree.
Amid errant flurries, we sing aloud,
In whimsical moments, we feel so proud.

Threads of Ice in a Woven Tale

Amidst the pines, the victory calls,
Snowflakes weave through all the brawls.
A slippery path, who takes the lead?
With giggles abound, we plant the seed.

A snowman grins, well out of place,
His button eyes wear a charming face.
We tiptoe past with whispered glee,
Daring fate in this frosty spree.

With every stumble, we dance the night,
As warmth and cold join in their fight.
In icy threads, our stories spin,
A tapestry of mishaps we wear like skin.

So here’s to winter, let laughter prevail,
In the threads of ice, we craft our tale.
Within this world of silly dreams,
We brush the frost and share our schemes.

Flakes of Fate in a Wintry Dance

Flakes whirled about in a playful spree,
They tumbled and twirled like wild jubilee.
With laughter and giggles, they graced the ground,
Creating a chaos that spun all around.

A snowball flew fast, a mischievous throw,
It caught a poor fellow, down he did go!
With shouts of delight, they all gathered near,
In this winter wonder, there's naught to fear.

Frosty flakes landed on noses and hats,
Chill met the chuckles, like cats with their spats.
Bundle up tightly, oh what a sight,
As flakes danced in glee, under the moonlight.

Even the trees wore a coat of pure white,
They whispered their secrets in the dim twilight.
So raise up your mugs, let the laughter ignite,
In this fest of the flakes, everything feels right.

Glacial Secrets and Silent Screams

The chill in the air holds secrets untold,
Yet laughter erupts as the stories unfold.
Snowmen arise with their carrot-like noses,
In poses so silly, like garden faux roses.

Muffled joys under blankets of white,
Echo through valleys, a soft, merry sight.
A family of snowmen armed with a grin,
Comically plotting a snowball to win.

Glistening surfaces hide giggles underneath,
The ice holds the pulse of this frosty wreath.
With squeals and splashes, the sleds race down,
Each crash and collapse brings laughter around.

Though winter can chill and bring moments of dread,
The fun never falters; we forge ahead.
From glacial whispers to joyful acclaim,
In this winter theater, we play our own game.

A Tenuous Truce in White Blanket

Under a blanket so soft and so bright,
A war rages on, but it feels just right.
Two factions collide with a snowball in hand,
Laughter erupts as they make their last stand.

They build their fortresses, tall and proud,
While plotting their sneaks beneath the white cloud.
A truce is declared, if just for a time,
As giggles and grunts mix in winter's rhyme.

Fluffy white creatures begin to appear,
With igloos and tunnels, our joy sincere.
We join in the fun, though rivalry brews,
In this flurry of fun, it’s hard to lose.

When the moon lights the scene, causing shadows to prance,
The laughter carries on, like a dance of chance.
Warmed by the thrill of a friendly act,
In this wintry playground, we made a pact.

The Storm's Tirade: Cold Emotions

A tempest approaches, winds howl and we shriek,
While outside it howls, it’s hilariously bleak.
The trees start to sway, a dance of despair,
Yet in this loud chaos, we find joy to share.

Icicles dangle like teeth from the eaves,
While we bundle up tight, in our long-sleeve sleeves.
Hot chocolate waits, with marshmallows afloat,
As nature throws tantrums, we sip and we gloat.

The storm's frosty fingers create a white mess,
Frosting the world in a chilling caress.
Yet each little flake brings a smile, not frowns,
As we brave the tempest, in our cozy town.

So let the winds howl and snowflakes parade,
We'll meet every gust with our laughter displayed.
For amidst all the drama, the cold and the heat,
In this wintry circus, our joy is complete.

Chilling Revelations

A snowman wearing shades, looking cool,
He tells me jokes that break all the rules.
The flakes fall down like silly confetti,
While penguins dance, oh so unsteady.

The sleds dash by, all in a race,
But one hits a bump, oh what a face!
Laughter echoes through the frosty night,
As bundled-up kids take to flight.

The dog leaps high, catches a snowball,
As logs in the fire start to enthrall.
Hot cocoa spills, a marshmallow fight,
With giggles that spark like stars in the night.

Icicles hang like teeth of a beast,
But we share a feast, winter's grand feast.
With every slip, tumble, and fall,
This chilly time brings joy to us all.

Glimmering Secrets

The moonlight shines on the frozen lake,
Where shadows dance, making me shake.
I saw a snowflake burst into song,
Telling tales that can't be wrong.

Glistening branches crack with delight,
While squirrels plot under the pale light.
Each fluff of snow hides stories untold,
Of snowball fights and wild kids bold.

Beneath the frost, secrets abound,
A whole world of fun waiting to be found.
With every wink of the twinkling stars,
Adventures await, lifting our bars.

Laughter rings through the icy air,
In this wonderland without a care.
Oh, these glimmering secrets we share,
Turn winter's chill into giggles and flair!

Winter's Bitter Sweetness

A candy cane sleigh, oh what a sight,
With gummy bears racing, full of delight.
We trip on our boots, giggling out loud,
As old men in scarves shuffle, feeling proud.

The cinnamon rolls topple from the plate,
As we fumble and laugh at our own fate.
A snowball flings, hits Dad in the nose,
His grumpy glare, cuter than a rose.

Building a fort that's grand and tall,
Yet one rogue snowball brings it all to a fall.
Winter is bittersweet, that is a fact,
But every mishap makes joy attract.

The sun dips low, the day's nearly done,
With frozen fingers, we frolic and run.
Sweetness of laughter in winter's fray,
Makes every mishap a holiday play.

Tides of Tempestuous Frost

The winter winds roar like a big old cat,
Bringing chilly tales that make me pat.
A snowball duel right in the street,
Where best buddies cry out, 'Take a seat!'

With every gust, hats fly to the sky,
While laughter erupts like the birds who fly.
The ice rink glimmers, a delight to behold,
But one wrong step leaves its stories told.

Frosty drip-drips make puddles galore,
As we slide and tumble, what a chore!
Yet every slip turns into a cheer,
With squeals of laughter ring loud and clear.

As flakes swirl in chaos, we dance around,
Our hearts like snowflakes, delightful and bound.
These tides of frost bring joy to unfold,
With winter's embrace, our spirits are bold.

Milton Keynes UK
Ingram Content Group UK Ltd.
UKHW022117251124
451529UK00012B/561

9 789916 942055